MW01503377

MADELINE SPENCER

A Pocket Guide to Siena, Italy

10 Essential Activities in Tuscany's Medieval Gem

First edition

This book was professionally typeset on Reedsy.
Find out more at reedsy.com

Contents

Acknowledgments

To my mom, whose unwavering belief in me gave me the confidence to chase this dream, and whose endless support made it possible. Thank you for always encouraging me to tell my stories.

and

To my wonderful husband — my anchor, best friend, and greatest adventure.

Introduction

Siena. Often labeled as a day trip from Florence, it's so much more than a quick stopover. There's a magic all its own in the air here, something intangible yet undeniably present. Maybe it's the way the golden light catches on the bricks of the piazza, or how the distant rolling hills seem to fold the city into the heart of Tuscany itself. Whatever it is, Siena leaves a mark on those who visit, and I was certainly no exception.

Siena is remarkably well-preserved, a city where history doesn't just sit behind museum glass. It lives and breathes in every corner. Walking through its gates feels like stepping into a piece of the past, yet despite its ancient roots, Siena is anything but a relic. The city is vibrant, filled with a strong, enduring sense of community and a deep pride that radiates from every piece of weathered stone.

I've been lucky enough to call Siena home for nearly five years now. As an American who came here with a tourist's wide eyes and fell deeply in love, I've had the rare privilege of experiencing this magical city from both perspectives. I've walked its streets as an awestruck visitor and wandered them as a resident finding my rhythm in its daily life. This dual perspective gives me a unique lens through which to share Siena with you, one that blends fresh wonder with the deeper appreciation that comes from living here.

The recommendations in this guide reflect my personal experiences and my ongoing love affair with Siena. Yes, some may be on the well-trodden tourist path, but as people sometimes say, things are touristy for a reason. These are must-sees and must-dos that capture the essence of Siena, the moments that leave an imprint on your heart and make you want to return again and again to dig deeper.

As you've already seen in the title, this is a starter guide — an introduction to Siena's magic and 10 essential activities to immerse yourself in the city's history, culture, and beauty. There's so much more I wanted to include, but to stay true to the "pocket guide" theme, I've kept things concise. If you find yourself wanting more, don't worry; this series will grow to explore each of these topics (and others) in much greater depth.

You can't (nor should you) squeeze all of these activities into one day, so I recommend picking what piques your interest or, better yet, extending your stay to take in all the highlights while immersing yourself in Siena's quotidian atmosphere. No matter how long you stay, my goal is to help you experience Siena in a way that goes beyond a simple checklist, so you not only see its most famous sights but also feel its rhythm and enduring spirit.

By the end of this book, you'll not only have a list of essential activities but also a sense of Siena's soul — its age-old traditions, vibrant culture, and timeless beauty. So, let's take your first step together through the gates into this enchanting, storied city. You just may end up falling in love with it, just like I did.

A Map of Siena's Historic Center

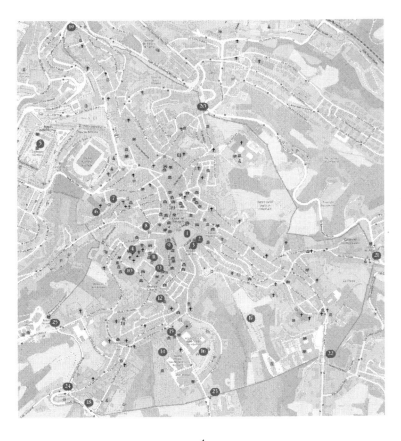

Map Legend

1 – Piazza del Campo

  2 – Torre del Mangia

  3 – Palazzo Pubblico (Museo Civico)

  4 – Duomo di Siena

  5 – Fortezza Medicea

  6 – Basilica Cateriniana di San Domenico

  7 – Panoramic City View (Via del Camporegio)

  8 – View of San Domenico (Via di Diacceto)

  9 – Museo della Tortura

10 – Santa Maria della Scala

11 – Museo dell'Opera

12 – Pinacoteca Nazionale di Siena

13 – Palazzo delle Papesse

14 – Orto Botanico

15 – Accademia dei Fisiocritici

16 – Orti dei Tolomei

17 – Orto de' Pecci

18 – Countryside Viewpoint (Via delle Sperandie)

19 – Porta Camollia

20 – Porta Ovile

21 – Porta Pispini

22 – Porta Romana
23 – Porta Tufi
24 – Porta San Marco
25 – Porta Laterina

Know Before You Go: Practical Tips

Of course, no travel guide is complete without some helpful tips to start you off. I'll keep it brief, but I wanted to provide some essentials to set you up for a smoother experience.

When to Visit

The Best Seasons

Early fall (late September to October) or late spring (end of April to early May) are some of my favorite times of year in Siena, as they offer mild weather and smaller crowds compared to peak summer. You may get occasional rain, but it only adds to Siena's medieval ambiance. And personally, I'd take some rain and pleasant temperatures over the crowds and suffocating heat of peak summer.

Winter Magic

Don't dismiss winter, either. It's the least crowded time of year, when the city fills with students from abroad rather than day-trippers, and the city's festive charm during the holiday season is as magical as you'd expect from a Tuscan town. With lights strung up around the central part of town, plus a dazzling Christmas tree, Siena feels cozier and more intimate this time of year.

When to Explore

Of course, some aspects of summer inevitably draw in visitors, and rightly so. The Palio, for example, occurs during summer's hottest months, but it's an unforgettable experience worth toughing out the blazing heat.

If you do choose to visit this time of year, keep your more active outings to the morning or evening. The stone streets and towering walls seem to trap the hot air, making midday a great time to retreat to a shady bar with a cold drink, indulge in some gelato, or explore one of Siena's hidden green spaces.

Getting Around

Siena's historic center is compact and very walking-friendly. That said, the hills and cobblestones can be challenging. While I've done my fair share of walking in heels, they aren't ideal for long walks (save them for a night out). Comfortable shoes are a must if you're planning a full day of exploration.

Pro Tip!

Siena's historic center isn't huge. You could walk between its furthest points in about 30-40 minutes. However, the quaint winding streets — my, and I'm sure many others', favorite part of smaller Italian towns — can get confusing if you aren't familiar with them.

Luckily, the central **Torre del Mangia** (the main city tower) and **campanile del Duomo** (the main cathedral's bell tower) are visible from many points in the city. Use the towers to orient yourself, or walk inward from the exterior walls. The **porte** (the main entrances of the historic center) are connected to the larger streets, which should bring you back to the central areas. You could also look at a map, but why not get a little lost?

Visit With Courtesy

While exploring, remember that Siena, like any other city, is alive. Locals work and go about their daily lives here. Be respectful, avoid loud behavior, pick up your trash, and treat the city with care to preserve its beauty for generations to come.

Activity 1: Soak in the Magic of the Piazza del Campo

The Florentine may disagree, but to me, Siena is the heart of Tuscany. And if Siena is the heart of Tuscany, the Piazza del Campo is the heart of Siena. Often referred to as simply **la piazza**, this iconic square is a marvel of medieval design and the centerpiece of the city's life and culture.

Piazza del Campo with a view of the Torre del Mangia and Palazzo Pubblico (on the right).

A Piazza Like No Other

While piazza is often translated to "square," the Piazza del Campo defies the usual geometric expectations. Unlike the more angular **piazze** of many historic centers, this piazza was designed with a unique shell-like formation, a deliberate and symbolic choice made by Siena's rulers, the Government of Nine, in 1297. Positioned at the convergence of three major roads, the piazza was envisioned as a communal space, open to all and free from religious or aristocratic dominance.

The rulers divided the square into nine sections to honor their government, often considered one of the most stable and peaceful in Siena's (and Italy's) history. The red brick pavement, laid in a stunning herringbone pattern and outlined by white travertine lines, adds to its beauty, while the surrounding medieval **palazzi** create an almost theatrical backdrop. Over the centuries, this stage filled the need for a space to host festivals, house merchants, and serve as a setting for political events. And, though time has passed, its function has changed very little.

Life in the Piazza Today

Today, Piazza del Campo remains the beating heart of Siena, where both locals and visitors gather to relax, celebrate, and soak in the city's rhythm. Twice a year, the Palio, Siena's legendary horse race, transforms the square into an electrifying amphitheater of competition and tradition. The energy is unmatched, with thousands crowding the piazza to watch as ten horses, each representing a **contrada** (district), race not just for victory but for honor, legacy, and the pride of their community.

But no matter the season, the piazza remains a centerpiece of daily life. If it's not host to the Palio, concerts, festivals, or the annual Christmas market, it hums with the rhythm of the everyday— children chasing pigeons, friends chatting over coffee, couples strolling hand in hand, and travelers pausing to marvel at the grandeur of the Torre del Mangia and the Palazzo Pubblico.

It's a living, breathing hub where the past and present merge seamlessly. Whether you're witnessing a grand celebration or simply enjoying a peaceful morning, Piazza del Campo offers a glimpse into the soul of Siena.

How to Experience the Piazza del Campo

The magic of Piazza del Campo isn't just in its history or architecture. It's in the way it makes you feel. I was once told that you only step into the piazza for the first time once, and every time after that just won't be as memorable. And while there may be some truth in that, I don't believe the magic ever fades. No matter how often I enter, I still feel a rush of wonder as I pass through one of the arched **portici** and watch the square reveal itself before me. The Torre del Mangia grows taller with every step, the space opens like a grand stage, inviting you to come and soak up its atmosphere.

While I wouldn't recommend sitting down for dinner at one of the **ristoranti** around the square (prices can be steep, and the food quality can be underwhelming), you can't go wrong grabbing a table at one of the many bars for an evening **aperitivo**. As the sun dips lower, the piazza flows with a warm, golden light, and the chatter of locals mixes with the hum of tourists. In summer, look to the skies at sunset to watch the swallows perform their mesmerizing aerial dances.

For a more casual experience, grab a gelato or a cold beer and find a spot to sit on the bricks. Take in the grandeur of the Palazzo Pubblico and the Torre del Mangia watching over you. It's the perfect place to pause, reflect, and feel the city's pulse.

Pro Tip!

While it's encouraged to sit and soak in the atmosphere, avoid lying down on the piazza's bricks. You may get a gentle scolding from the local authorities who roam the area on busier days. Also, keep food to a minimum. Gelato is perfect, but I've been told I have to eat my **panino** standing up (though other times it hasn't been an issue). To be on the safe side, enjoy a quick snack here, but save your full meal for an **osteria** tucked away in Siena's charming side streets.

Activity 2: Climb the Torre del Mangia

Standing tall over Piazza del Campo, the Torre del Mangia is one of, if not the, most iconic landmark in Siena. Rising 87 meters (around 285 feet), this medieval tower offers not only a glimpse into Siena's past but also the most breathtaking panoramic views of the city and surrounding countryside. Climbing its steps, following the footprints of countless others who came before, is a physical challenge for some — but an unforgettable experience for all.

View of the Torre del Mangia from the Cortile del Podestà, where you'll find the ticket office.

A Tower Rooted in History

While some sources suggest that work officially began in 1338 with the first recorded payment, others propose that construction was underway by 1325, with completion between 1344 and 1348. Regardless of the exact date, the tower was built as a bold statement of Siena's civic pride, celebrating the city's independence and defiance against feudal rule. Despite starting from a lower elevation, its height exceeds that of the Duomo's bell tower and is frequently interpreted as a symbol of balance between religious and secular authority. Even today, it remains one of the tallest historic towers in Italy, a testament to Siena's once-powerful republic and its enduring legacy.

For many, however, the tower's most intriguing detail is its name — Torre del Mangia (literally, "Tower of the Eater"). This odd title comes from its first bell-ringer, Giovanni di Balducci, nicknamed **mangiaguadagni** (or "profit-eater") thanks to his reputation for squandering money. The name stuck, and the Torre del Mangia continues to intrigue visitors with its curious moniker.

The Climbing Experience

Climbing the Torre del Mangia is an adventure in itself. With around 400 steps, the medieval staircase can feel steep and claustrophobic at times, but small openings along the way provide fleeting glimpses of the city below — a visual reward and a moment to catch your breath.

At the summit, the effort is richly rewarded. The Piazza del Campo unfolds beneath you, its shell-shaped design more evident from this elevated perspective. Beyond Siena's red rooftops, the rolling Chianti hills stretch endlessly, forming the picture-perfect Tuscan landscape that so many dream of when they imagine this region (I know I sure did!).

Tickets & Practical Tips

Tickets

To purchase tickets, enter through the door just to the right of the tower in the Palazzo Pubblico. You'll enter the Cortile del Podestà, where the ticket office is located. The office is open most days.

- *November 1 to February 28: Open 10:00 AM – 4:00 PM (with a short closing break from 1:00 PM – 1:45 PM).*
- *March 1 to October 31: Open 10:00 AM – 7:00 PM (with a short closing break from 1:45 PM – 2:30 PM).*

Ticket bundles are available for the tower and other key museums (Museo Civico and Santa Maria della Scala).

Best Times to Visit

For the clearest vistas, aim to climb the tower on a sunny day, ideally in the morning or late afternoon when the crowds are thinner and the light is softer.

ACTIVITY 2: CLIMB THE TORRE DEL MANGIA

Managing the Climb

The staircase is steep and narrow with uneven, slippery steps, so be prepared for a bit of exertion. Wear comfortable shoes and take your time. Note that the climb may not be suitable for those with mobility issues or a fear of heights.

Activity 3: Marvel at the Duomo's Gothic Splendor

If there's one sight in Siena that truly takes my breath away no matter how many times I visit, it's the Duomo di Siena. Yes, it's a "touristy" spot, but for good reason. Its stunning architecture, intricate details, and rich history make it a must-see for anyone visiting the city. Whether it's your first time or your fiftieth, the Duomo never fails to inspire awe.

Close-up view of the cathedral's front facade, tower, and dome.

A Monument to Faith, Power, and Artistry

Construction of the Duomo began in the 13th century on the site of an old church dedicated to the Virgin Mary and, before that, a temple dedicated to Minerva. Siena's rulers envisioned a cathedral that would not only serve as a religious landmark but also as a symbol of the city's wealth and artistic ambition.

The original plan was grand; However, financial struggles and the devastation of the Black Death in 1348 halted expansion, leaving behind what is now known as the **facciatone**, an

unfinished facade of the intended grander cathedral. While
was never completed as planned, what remains is nothing short
of magnificent. You can even walk along the facciatone, which
now serves as one of the best panoramic viewpoints in the city.

The Cathedral's Key Features

Il Pavimento: The Marble Mosaic Floor

Giorgio Vasari, a renowned Italian painter, architect, and
historian, once described it as the "most beautiful . . .,
largest and most magnificent floor ever made." This intricate
masterpiece comprises 56 panels depicting biblical scenes and
allegories, crafted by various artists over six centuries using the
graffito and marble inlay technique. I've been fortunate to see
them a handful of times, and the detail and artistry continue to
astonish me. This Duomo tells many of its stories underfoot,
the inlays conveying centuries of devotion in a way that feels
personal yet magnificently grand.

Important note: The floor is often covered for protection and is
only fully unveiled during specific times of the year, typically
from late June to late July and mid-August to mid-October.

Piccolomini Library: A Renaissance Jewel

Commissioned by Cardinal Francesco Piccolomini (later Pope Pius III) to honor his uncle, Pope Pius II, the Piccolomini Library is a masterpiece of Renaissance artistry. Its vaulted ceiling is alive with allegorical figures, pastoral scenes, and Bacchic celebrations, while the walls' frescoes recount the life of Pius II — from his early days as a scholar and diplomat to his rise as pope. Now filled with illuminated manuscripts, the library is one of Siena's greatest artistic treasures. No matter how many times I visit, I can't help but smile in awe, as if I'm seeing it for the first time.

Gothic Grandeur: The Facade and Interior

A striking example of Romanesque-Gothic design, the cathedral features black and white stripes of marble, the colors of Siena's coat of arms. Intricate carvings, statues, and ornate details cover every inch, one of my favorites being the interior's star-speckled royal blue ceiling. During times of the year when the central flooring is covered, you can walk right under the dome and admire the grand scale of the cathedral from a different perspective. I love to stand in the center and look upward, imagining the countless others who have gazed in awe.

Tickets & Practical Tips

Ticket Options

The OPA Si Pass grants access to multiple sites within the Duomo complex, including the Cathedral, Piccolomini Library, Museo dell'Opera, Panorama, Crypt, and Baptistery. This pass is valid for three consecutive days, making it a great choice for those who want to explore at a leisurely pace.

- *Standard tickets for just the Cathedral and Library are also available if you prefer a shorter visit.*
- *The Porta del Cielo Tour gives visitors access to the cathedral's rooftop walkways, providing a unique perspective of both the interior and the city below. These tickets require advanced booking and are time-slot specific.*

When to Visit

To avoid crowds, plan your visit right around lunchtime or late in the afternoon.

If you don't mind the busier season, in 2025, the **pavimento** will be uncovered from:

- *June 27 – July 31 and August 18 – October 15*

Allow enough time to explore all parts of the complex. While it's possible to see the highlights in a couple of hours, setting aside half a day ensures you can fully appreciate the cathedral's beauty and history without feeling rushed.

Activity 4: Discover the Culture of the Contrade

Siena is a city of deep-rooted traditions, and nothing embodies its spirit more than its **contrade**. These 17 districts, each with its own identity, history, and symbolism, are the lifeblood of Siena's culture. To understand Siena is to understand the contrade (and their most famous event, the Palio di Siena). As my husband and I often note, without the contrade, without the Palio, there is no Siena.

Bruco contrada during the race day ceremonies. Pairs from each contrada compete for best performance.

The Palio: Siena's Living History

The Palio di Siena is a historic horse race held twice a year in the iconic Piazza del Campo — on July 2nd and August 16th. This thrilling event features ten of the 17 contrade, selected through a rotating system and a lottery. Far more than a race, the Palio is a vivid expression of Siena's historical rivalries and communal pride.

The Palio traces its origins back to the Middle Ages when it

29

emerged from military drills and public games before gradually evolving into a structured competition. It first took the form of a buffalo race, but in the latter half of the 17th century, it transformed into the horse race we know today. Victory in the Palio brings immense honor, and the celebrations (or heartbreak) last long after the race has ended. For Sienese residents, the Palio is not just a two-day affair—it's the thread that weaves together the city's cultural fabric, with preparations and strategic discussions spanning the entire year.

Having been in the **piazza** a handful of times to witness the Palio, I can tell you it's a profoundly emotional experience. The energy is palpable. Thousands of people stand shoulder to shoulder, yet as the horses begin to line up, the crowd falls into an eerie, absolute silence — a collective breath held in anticipation. Then, after what could be either minutes or hours, the race begins.

After the horses make their three quick laps around the piazza, you'll see people of all ages shedding tears of joy or defeat. It's a spectacle of passion that words can barely capture.

A Neighborhood Affair

The contrade, also with medieval origins, began as topographical references or markers rather than structured entities. Over time, these districts evolved into close-knit communities with unique identities and emblems, such as the Giraffe, the Snail, and the Dragon.

The number of contrade has fluctuated over the centuries due to urban changes, economic shifts, and historical events like the Black Death, finally stabilizing in the 16th century into the 17 districts recognized today. Each contrada now functions as a mini-community, complete with its own museum, church, and social events. Though there are some exceptions, membership is typically hereditary; children are "baptized" into the same contrada as their parents, fostering a strong sense of belonging among the members.

One of the most intriguing aspects of the contrade is their fierce loyalty and rivalry (for example, the Leocorno and Civetta contrade are historic rivals). Alliances are forged and broken, old feuds resurface, and strategies unfold not just on the track but throughout the entire year. Yet beyond the politics of it all, the contrade serve as a cornerstone of community life, hosting events, celebrations, and activities that bring the city to life.

The 17 contrade: Aquila (eagle), Chiocciola (snail), Onda (wave), Pantera (panther), Selva (forest), Tartuca (turtle), Civetta (owl), Leocorno (unicorn), Nicchio (seashell), Torre (tower), Valdimontone (ram), Bruco (caterpillar), Drago (dragon), Giraffa (giraffe), Istrice (porcupine), Lupa (she-wolf), Oca (goose)

A Window Into Contrada Culture

For visitors, exploring the contrade offers a unique window into Siena's heart and soul. Here are two ways to immerse yourself:

Visit the Contrade Museums

Each contrada has a museum where you can learn about its history, see its winning Palio banners, and admire artifacts that tell the story of its community. These museums are a treasure trove of Sienese culture and a must-see for anyone wanting to delve deeper into the city's traditions. Check with the local tourist office or visit individual contrade websites. Most have email addresses you can contact for bookings.

Note: The contrade websites will likely not have an English language option. To locate the email addresses, look for **museo** (museum) or **contatti** (contacts) in the navigation menu.

Spot the Contrade Fountains

As you wander Siena's streets, challenge yourself to find all 17 contrade fountains, each uniquely designed to represent its district's emblem. This scavenger hunt-style activity is a fun way to engage with the city's history, architecture, and Tuscan charm while appreciating the pride and tradition of each contrada.

Pro Tip!

As you walk through Siena, you can determine which contrada you're in by spotting its emblem on the walls of the surrounding buildings. Each district proudly displays its colors and symbol, often carved into stone or affixed as plaques. During the summer, you'll also notice ornate lamps lining the streets, further marking the boundaries of each contrada.

Activity 5: Walk the Fortezza Medicea

Standing as both a symbol of Siena's turbulent history and its vibrant present, the **Fortezza Medicea** offers visitors a chance to explore a site where history, community, and breathtaking views converge. Built by the Medici family as a military fortress, it now serves as a beloved gathering place for locals and tourists alike.

A ground-level view of a fort bastion featuring the Medici crest.

From Military Stronghold to Community Space

The Fortezza Medicea was constructed in the mid-16th century after the fall of the Republic of Siena. Following Florence's defeat of Siena in 1555, the Medici rulers ordered the fortress to be built as a means of asserting control over the rebellious city. While its strategic location was primarily defensive, the fortress, as a constant reminder of Florentine dominance over Siena, also served as a statement of Medici authority.

Over time, the fortress transitioned from a symbol of war and oppression to a community hub. Today, the Fortezza Medicea, referred to by locals as simply **la fortezza**, serves as a venue for events, recreation, and cultural activities and is a beloved spot in the community.

Things to Do at the Fortezza

Take in the Views

Stroll along the fortress's historic ramparts to enjoy panoramic views of Siena and the surrounding countryside. The vistas are especially stunning at sunset, when the golden light bathes the rolling hills and rooftops of the city. The Duomo, with its striking black and white stripes and soaring **campanile**, stands out boldly against Siena's terracotta rooftops and the expansive blue sky.

Attend Events

During the summer months, the fortress comes alive with activity. A seasonal bar is often set up within its walls, offering live music and a lively atmosphere. It's a wonderful place to mingle with locals and enjoy the city's vibrant social life. Additional events, such as outdoor cinema screenings or winter ice skating, make the fortress a year-round attraction.

Though not in the fortress itself, there is also a weekly market every Wednesday morning along the streets just outside. This bustling market is a favorite among both locals and visitors and offers everything from fresh produce and flowers to clothing and household items. It's a lively and colorful experience that perfectly complements a visit to the fort. My husband and I will often go to grab some fresh roses and a roast chicken!

Get Active

The open spaces within the fortress are perfect for exercise. You'll find basic workout equipment atop one of the four historic bastions, or you can simply jog or walk the ramparts for a scenic workout. You'll often spot locals incorporating the fortress into their daily routines.

Practical Tips

When to Go

The fort is open every day, year-round. I find early mornings and evenings particularly magical, no matter the time of year.

What to Bring

Wear comfortable shoes for walking and bring a camera to capture the incredible views. Grab some food and drink as well if you want to enjoy a casual lunch shaded under the trees.

Fort Access

The fortress is free to enter and easily accessible from the city center, making it a convenient (and essential!) stop during your exploration.

Activity 6: Savor the Flavors of Siena

Siena's culinary traditions are as rich and layered as its history. Rooted in simplicity and a deep connection to the land, the city's cuisine offers a window into the heart of Tuscan life. From hearty soups to sweet treats, eating in Siena is a journey through flavors that have been cherished for centuries.

Pici al cinghiale, a personal favorite of mine.

Siena's Food Culture and History

Siena's food culture is grounded in tradition and resourceful-ness. Tuscan cuisine, in general, is known for its simplicity, focusing on high-quality, seasonal ingredients rather than elaborate techniques. Siena is no exception, with dishes that reflect the region's agricultural heritage and meals that are hearty, flavorful, and deeply satisfying.

Dining in Siena (and in Italy as a whole) is an entire experience in and of itself. Meals tend to be leisurely affairs, often accompanied by conversation and, of course, wine. Seasonal menus dominate, with dishes changing to reflect the best ingredients of the moment, from winter's hearty stews to summer's lighter fare.

Dining Options

When dining, you'll encounter a variety of establishments, each offering its own twist on local cuisine.

Osteria: Traditionally, these spots are wine-focused, with just simple items to snack on. Modern **osterie** are usually casual establishments with a full menu and curated wine selection.

Trattoria: A trattoria is generally even more casual and more food-focused than an osteria, often with extensive menus and greater emphasis on traditional Tuscan dishes.

Ristorante: A bit more formal than the others, **ristoranti** are ideal for when you're craving a more elevated dining experience. They offer a more "refined" menu and extra-attentive service.

Pro Tip!

You'll find a red and white **vino della casa** (house wine) in nearly every osteria or trattoria. It's perfect for when you want something extra affordable that still tastes great with the meal (*Bonus*: You can order in large quantities without breaking the bank. Grab a liter (or two) to share with the table!).

Must-Try Dishes and Ingredients

No trip to Siena is complete without sampling its culinary treasures. Here are some must-try items.

Savory

Pici: Thick, hand-rolled pasta native to Siena. Try it:

- *All'aglione*: A tomato and "big garlic" sauce.
- *Al cinghiale*: A rich sauce made with wild boar.
- *Al ragù di cinta senese:* A white ragù made with prized local pig known for its flavorful meat.

Ribollita: A vegetable and bread soup, traditionally made with leftovers. Perfect for warming up on a chilly winter day.

Sweet

Ricciarelli: Almond cookies with a soft, chewy texture, dusted with powdered sugar. A personal favorite!

Panforte: A dense, spiced fruit and nut cake. Though originally a Christmas treat, it's enjoyed year-round.

Restaurant Recommendations

I'll admit it: There are still many restaurants on my to-eat-at list, but here are some that my husband, our friends, and I love to return to again and again.

Osteria Da Gano: A welcoming osteria offering traditional dishes at very reasonable prices.

La Compagnia dei Vinattieri: A personal favorite ristorante with great food and an extensive wine selection.

Ristorante San Desiderio: More refined takes on Sienese classics in a casual atmosphere and beautiful setting (a deconsecrated Romanesque church!).

Osteria Da Divo: Though it has osteria in the name, this more ristorante-style spot offers an elevated dining experience set in an ancient Etruscan cave.

Gallo Nero: A higher-end restaurant in what was once a medieval mansion. They offer a blend of traditional Tuscan flavors and contemporary twists.

Dining Hours

Dining times in Siena follow the traditional Italian schedule, which may be different from what visitors are used to.

Lunch

Typically served between 12:00 PM – 3:00 PM, though many locals eat closer to 1:00 PM – 2:00 PM. After 3:00 PM, most restaurants close for a few hours.

Keep in mind that many waitstaff work long shifts and have only a short break before returning for the evening service, so be mindful of dining hours. In other words, try not to show up at 2:50!

Dinner

Restaurant kitchens usually reopen around 7:00 PM – 7:30 PM, but locals tend to dine later, around 8:00 PM – 9:30 PM.

Pro Tip!

If you're hungry outside of these hours, there are many **panini** shops around town that are open throughout the day. Many bars (café-like establishments with coffee, drinks, and smaller bites) also stay open, making them a great option for a quick snack or a light meal.

Activity 7: Visit a Museum

Siena's charm isn't just found in its medieval streets and breath-taking views. It's also housed within its many museums, where the city's rich history, art, and culture are preserved. From grand collections of Renaissance masterpieces to fascinating scientific curiosities, Siena offers a diverse range of museums that cater to every interest.

While there are plenty of small exhibition halls and historic rooms to explore, this chapter focuses on a few of Siena's more comprehensive museums — where you can spend an hour or two fully immersed in the city's past.

Pellegrinaio hall, founded as a refuge for pilgrims in the 12th century.

Museo dell'Opera del Duomo

If you're captivated by the grandeur of Siena's Duomo, then the Museo dell'Opera del Duomo is a must-visit. Part of the Duomo "complex," this museum houses many of the cathedral's original sculptures, artworks, and stained glass windows that were removed for preservation.

One of its most famous pieces is Duccio di Buoninsegna's Maestà, a masterpiece of Sienese Gothic art that once adorned the cathedral's high altar. You'll also find an impressive collection of sculptures by Giovanni Pisano, whose intricate carvings once decorated the cathedral's facade.

And, if I haven't mentioned it enough, don't miss the chance to climb to the facciatone, the unfinished facade of what was meant to be Siena's expanded cathedral. From here, you'll get one of the city's best panoramic views.

Museo Civico (Palazzo Pubblico)

Located inside the Palazzo Pubblico, Siena's historic town hall, the Museo Civico is one of the city's most significant museums. It is home to some of Siena's most celebrated frescoes, including The Allegory of Good and Bad Government by Ambrogio Lorenzetti—a powerful visual representation of justice and corruption that still resonates today. Other highlights include Simone Martini's Maestà, a stunning Gothic depiction of the

Virgin Mary, and the intricate decorations of the Sala dei Nove, the council room of Siena's medieval government.

While the Museo dell'Opera del Duomo offers insight into Siena's religious and artistic heritage, the Museo Civico provides a window into the city's political past, showcasing the ideals, struggles, and governance of Siena's medieval republic.

Pinacoteca Nazionale di Siena

Tucked away on a quiet stretch of Via San Pietro, the Pinacoteca Nazionale is a treasure trove of Sienese painting and a must for art lovers. Housed within two adjoining Gothic palaces—the Palazzo Buonsignori and Palazzo Brigidi—it holds one of Italy's most important collections of medieval and early Renaissance art.

Room by room, the museum traces Siena's artistic golden age. The collection spans the 13th to 16th centuries, showcasing the refined elegance of the Sienese School. Expect luminous gold backgrounds, bold colorways, and spiritual intensity in works by Duccio di Buoninsegna, Simone Martini, the Lorenzetti brothers, and other local masters who helped define Gothic art in Europe.

What makes the Pinacoteca (and most museums in Siena, for that matter) especially compelling is its emphasis on local identity. Unlike larger, pan-Italian museums, this one feels deeply rooted in place. Many of the altarpieces and panels on display were originally commissioned for Siena's churches and

49

civic buildings, meaning you're seeing integral parts of the city's religious and cultural fabric.

Don't miss the upper floor, where later Renaissance works begin to show a shift toward more naturalistic styles—marking the slow turn away from the Gothic tradition. It's a fascinating contrast and adds depth to your understanding of the artistic evolution that took place in Siena.

Though the museum is relatively quiet compared to Siena's more central attractions, that's part of its charm. A visit here offers a contemplative, almost reverent atmosphere. Give yourself at least an hour to explore, though true art lovers may want even more time to savor the details.

Santa Maria della Scala

Perhaps my favorite museum of the city, Santa Maria della Scala, located directly across from the Duomo, was once one of the oldest hospitals in Europe. Founded in the 12th century, it served as a refuge for pilgrims, the sick, and the poor, and over the centuries, it expanded into what is now one of the city's most fascinating museums — a vast network of chapels, frescoed halls, and underground tunnels that provide a rare glimpse into Siena's past.

Walking through Santa Maria della Scala is like peeling back layers of history. The Pellegrinaio, a grand hall that once housed the hospital's patients, is decorated with breathtaking frescoes depicting scenes of charity and care. Below, the archaeological museum houses an extensive collection of Etruscan and Roman artifacts, revealing Siena's ancient roots. Deeper still, underground tunnels lead to grain storage rooms and forgotten chambers.

Beyond its medical history, the complex also contains sacred spaces, including the Oratory of Santa Caterina della Notte, where Saint Catherine of Siena was said to have prayed and slept. Whether you're drawn to medieval art, archaeology, or simply the idea of stepping into a place where history was lived rather than just displayed, Santa Maria della Scala is an unmissable stop.

Note: If you plan to visit, set aside ample time to explore. The museum is expansive, and the archaeological section alone offers a wealth of artifacts and detailed signage worth lingering over. Even a rushed visit can take over an hour; if you want to fully appreciate the depth of history on display, plan for at least a few hours.

Accademia dei Fisiocritici

For something a little different, the Accademia dei Fisiocritici offers a fascinating look into natural history and science. One of the oldest scientific academies in Italy, this museum features a diverse collection of geological specimens, taxidermy animals, and even an entire whale skeleton.

The museum's name, Fisiocritici, roughly translates to "judges of nature," reflecting its founders' mission to explore and understand the natural world. Its eclectic collection is housed in a former Camaldolese monastery, adding an extra layer of history to your visit.

The museum is a few floors tall, and on each level, there are floor-to-ceiling glass cases packed with items — everything from minerals and fossils to preserved animals and anatomical specimens. It feels like stepping into an old-world cabinet of curiosities, a surprising and welcome departure from the museums you might expect to see. If you enjoy quirky museums with a mix of science and history, this hidden gem is well worth a stop.

Museo della Tortura

For those intrigued by Siena's darker history, the Museo della Tortura provides a chilling but educational look at medieval justice. This small museum showcases a collection of torture devices and methods once used in Europe, offering insight into the harsh realities of law enforcement in past centuries.

While not for the faint of heart, the museum is a fascinating exploration of how power and punishment were wielded in medieval society. If you enjoy offbeat museums, this one adds a very different perspective to your Siena experience.

Activity 8: Walk the Walls & Winding Streets

Siena's medieval walls are not only a testament to its rich history but also a unique way to explore the city's charm. These ancient fortifications, paired with Siena's enchanting streets, offer an unforgettable walking experience that reveals the city's character from a variety of perspectives.

A view of Porta Camollia and its Latin inscription.

A Brief History of Siena's "Mura"

The origins of Siena's walls date back to the early Middle Ages, when they were built to protect the once smaller, though growing, city from invasions. Over the centuries, the walls were continuously extended to encompass new districts, with the final major modifications completed in the 16th century. Today, they enclose the historic center, punctuated by imposing gates, or **porte**, that served as vital entry points for travelers and goods.

Originally built for military defense, Siena's walls played a crucial role in protecting the city, with Porta Camollia being one of the most heavily fortified due to its strategic position on the road from Florence. However, after Siena fell under Medici rule, the walls took on additional administrative functions, serving as customs checkpoints to regulate the city's trade and taxation. Today, Siena's walls and gates remain a defining feature of the city. Porta Camollia, once a defensive stronghold, now stands as a testament to Siena's welcoming spirit, bearing the Latin inscription *Cor magis tibi Sena pandit* ("Siena shows a heart bigger than this gate").

Meanwhile, the southern gates, historically connected Siena to the agricultural lands beyond, now serve as a gateway to the breathtaking **Crete Senesi** region. Though visitors can't walk directly on the walls, their imposing presence still shapes the city's skyline and offers countless scenic viewpoints.

Exploring Siena's Walls and Streets

You can't walk the full length of the walls, but several elevated paths and viewpoints allow you to see over them, offering sweeping panoramas of the city and the rolling Tuscan countryside beyond. Combine these vantage points with a stroll through Siena's winding streets for a walking experience that captures the city's variety.

One of my absolute favorite things to do in Siena is to go on these longer walks. There are endless routes to take, and you could easily spend an entire day meandering through the historic streets, but the areas I find myself drawn back to the most are the Tartuca, Chiocciola, and Pantera districts, leading toward Porta Tufi, Porta San Marco, and Porta Laterina. These areas tend to be quieter and more tucked away, making them perfect for escaping the crowds while still soaking in Siena's medieval charm.

Practical Walking Tips

Wear Comfortable Shoes: Siena's cobblestones and hilly terrain can be challenging, so sturdy footwear is essential if you'll be walking for extended amounts of time.

Bring Some Water: While there are plenty of cafés along the way, it never hurts to have some extra water on you, especially if you'll be visiting during summer.

Time Your Walk: Mornings and late afternoons are ideal for exploring, as you'll avoid the midday heat and enjoy softer lighting for photos.

Stay Aware of Traffic: Some streets are shared with vehicles, so keep an eye out when wandering.

Activity 9: Take in the Views

The top of the Torre del Mangia isn't the only place you'll find breathtaking views. Even after years of living here, I still catch myself stopping mid-walk, captivated by the city's beauty. Whether it's a panoramic vista of terracotta rooftops or the rolling Tuscan hills beyond, these vistas never lose their magic. They provide a chance to reflect, marvel at Siena's timeless beauty, and connect with the city in a more personal way.

Southeast view from the upper portion of the facciatone.

Ticketed Viewpoints for Siena's Best Panoramas

Facciatone

A must-visit for panoramic views, the **facciatone** is part of the unfinished expansion of the Siena Cathedral. Originally meant to be part of a grander basilica, it now serves as a sort of open-air balcony with breathtaking 360-degree views.

Torre del Mangia

The climb of around 400 steps is steep but rewarding, revealing a stunning bird's-eye view of the Duomo's striped marble facade, the maze of medieval streets, and the rolling hills beyond the city walls.

Porta del Cielo

You'll step through narrow passages, once used only by maintenance workers, to gain a unique aerial perspective of the Duomo's stunning interior. Up close, admire the intricate frescoes, soaring arches, and stunning vaulted ceiling before stepping outside to take in breathtaking panoramic views of Siena's skyline.

Palazzo delle Papesse

Located on Via di Città, one of the three principal streets in Siena's historic center, this former noble residence offers stunning terrace views overlooking the city's medieval rooftops. It now houses contemporary art exhibitions, but visitors can still access its beautiful vantage points.

Pinacoteca Nazionale

While best known for its medieval masterpieces, the Pinacoteca also surprises visitors with one of the most enchanting window views in the city. Tucked into one of the upper-floor galleries is a quiet room with a perfectly framed view of the Torre del Mangia rising above the rooftops.

Green Escapes: Siena's Most Peaceful Viewpoints

Fortezza Medicea Viewpoint

The Medici Fortress isn't just a historical site but also home to one of the best vantage points in Siena. From its elevated position, you can enjoy a long-distance view of the Duomo and the city's skyline. Below the fortress, there's a bar — separate from the one inside the park during summer — that offers the same breathtaking view, making it the perfect spot to sip a drink while taking in the scenery.

Orti dei Tolomei

For a quieter and more intimate perspective, head to the Orti dei Tolomei. This serene park offers a peaceful retreat from the city's hustle and bustle. From here, you can enjoy a unique view of Siena's back side and the rolling Tuscan hills beyond. It's an ideal spot for a leisurely stroll or a picnic.

Walking Views: Stunning Spots Along the Way

Via Camporegio

This is one of my favorite places to take in a panoramic view of Siena. The view offers a clear, relatively up-close perspective of the Duomo and Torre del Mangia rising above the terracotta rooftops. In the soft morning light or the golden glow of sunset (any time of day, really), the scene feels like a painting come to life.

Pro Tip!

Despite its central location, this spot tends to be less crowded than some of the city's other viewpoints, making it ideal for quiet reflection or photography. Take a seat on the bench on the raised terrace outside the San Domenico basilica, and watch as light illuminates Siena's shades of gold, terracotta, and crimson. It's a perfect spot to pause and take in the city's layered beauty.

Via di Diacceto

Via di Diacceto offers a gorgeous framed view of San Domenico, set against Siena's rooftops and greenery. Located just near the Duomo, it's a great stop while wandering through the city center, providing a unique angle of one of Siena's most striking landmarks.

Via delle Sperandie

A true hidden gem, Via delle Sperandie provides an unexpected but striking view of the city's surrounding hills. It's an ideal detour for those who enjoy wandering off the beaten path.

When I'm feeling particularly contemplative, this is the spot I'll visit. There's rarely other people who linger there, and the view seems to mirror that quiet mood—soft hills rolling into the horizon, a patchwork of fields, trees, and stone houses unfolding in gentle stillness. It's a place that naturally invites reflection.

Activity 10: Escape to Siena's Greener Side

One of my favorite things about Siena: You never know what's beyond each building. The city may be celebrated for its medieval stone architecture, but it also hides a surprising number of green spaces. From tranquil gardens to lush parks, these outdoor spots provide a refreshing contrast to Siena's historic streets.

A view from the Orto de' Pecci.

Unexpected Green Spaces

For a city known for its winding alleys and towering walls, Siena offers plenty of hidden green gems where you can slow down and breathe. These peaceful retreats are perfect for relaxing after a day of sightseeing or for connecting with Siena's quieter, natural side.

L'Orto Botanico

A peaceful escape in the heart of the city, and one of my favorite spots to visit, the botanical garden is a must-see for nature lovers. Its origins date back to the early 17th century, during which the Semplici Gardens were being cultivated near the Hospital Santa Maria della Scala for the study of medicinal plants. In 1784, the Grand Duke of Tuscany, Pietro Leopoldo, transformed it into the University Botanical Garden, emphasizing its role in scientific research. By 1856, the garden was moved to its current location near Porta Tufi, where it expanded to support education and conservation efforts.

The garden now spans 2.5 hectares and contains over 2,000 species of plants, including rare and endangered specimens. Divided into themed sections, it lets visitors explore Tuscany's various ecosystems, from the Tyrrhenian coastline to the iconic rolling hills. There are also dedicated areas for aquatic plants, succulents, and a fern forest. One of the most striking features is the 19th-century greenhouse (antica serra), built in 1875, which houses exotic plants from equatorial regions.

Whether you're a botany enthusiast or simply seeking a tranquil retreat, the Orto Botanico di Siena offers a unique blend of history, science, and natural beauty — hidden within the city's medieval walls.

L'Orto de' Pecci

Once a medieval vegetable garden, the Orto de' Pecci has a long, layered history. In the 14th century, people sentenced to death would pass through the now brick-filled Porta Giustizia (the "Door of Justice") on their way to execution, with the garden being one of the final spaces they walked through. Legend has it there's even a spirit (some say vampire) that inhabits the area.

Over the centuries, the garden took on new iterations, later becoming part of the Ospedale Psichiatrico (Psychiatric Hospital), where patients worked the land and cared for the animals as part of their rehabilitation. Even today, the garden serves a similar social function; it is run by **La Proposta**, a cooperative that began in the 1980s to help young unemployed individuals and former psychiatric patients find work. Over the years, it has become a respected institution that preserves the garden's history while giving back to the community.

For visitors, the Orto de' Pecci is a peaceful natural retreat just a short walk from Piazza del Campo. With its lush grassy meadow, fruit orchards, and lower-positioned views of Siena's medieval skyline, it offers a tranquil contrast to the bustling city center. It's my husband's and my go-to Sunday spot, perfect for relaxing and soaking in a different perspective of Siena.

Pro Tip!

There's a small restaurant in the park where you can enjoy a casual, traditional meal. It's a great place to experience Siena's countryside charm without leaving the city center.

Gli Orti dei Tolomei

Tucked near Porta Tufi, a few steps away from the Church of Sant'Agostino, the Orti dei Tolomei is a peaceful retreat hidden within Siena's city walls. Originally, this area was cultivated as vegetable gardens by the friars of the convent, but over time, it was transformed into a public green space. Today, it's one of the city's best-kept secrets, a spot known among locals but often overlooked by short-term visitors.

The park retains a serene and historic atmosphere, with shaded pathways, centuries-old olive trees, and breathtaking views of Siena's rolling countryside. One of its most striking features is "The Drop," a pear-shaped travertine sculpture commissioned by the Tartuca contrada.

It's a favorite among locals and students (and myself!) for its tranquility, fresh air, and picturesque scenery. Whether you want to unwind on a bench with a book, enjoy a leisurely walk, or simply take in the breathtaking view, Orti dei Tolomei is a perfect spot to escape the crowds.

Pro Tip!

Grab some **panini** from a nearby shop and stretch out under the olive trees. It's the perfect way to recharge before continuing your Siena adventure.

Conclusion

Siena is a city that lingers with you long after you've left. Its medieval streets, golden sunsets, and deep-rooted traditions leave a mark that doesn't seem to fade, a reminder and invitation for you to return. Whether this was your first glimpse into its wonders or another step in your journey of discovering Siena, I hope this guide has given you a sense of its magic and a desire to experience even more.

There's always more to uncover — hidden alleyways that reveal unexpected views and quiet moments of connection with the city's timeless soul. As this pocket guide has only scratched the surface, I encourage you to keep exploring, embrace Siena's slow rhythm, and let curiosity lead you beyond the well-known landmarks.

Siena is not a city to rush through; it's not simply a day trip from Florence but a place to wander without a destination, sit and watch the world go by, and get lost in its labyrinth of streets and find something unexpected. Each visit deepens your connection to the city to reveal something new. I first stepped foot through those medieval gateways seven years ago and have called Siena home for nearly five. Yet, I still find myself enchanted by small discoveries — an unfamiliar corner, a hidden courtyard, a local shop I hadn't noticed before. Even the grand sights continue to captivate me in new ways.

So, whether you're already planning your next trip or simply carrying a piece of Siena with you in your heart, I hope this guide has inspired you to experience the city not just as a visitor, but as someone who truly wants to connect with its history, culture, and beauty. Siena has a way of calling you back, and when it does, I hope you'll answer.

References

Berta, M. (2023, March 27). *The Contrade of Siena*. Terre Di Siena. https://www.terredisiena.it/en/siena-en/the-contrade-of-siena/

CATTEDRALE. (n.d.) Opera Duomo Siena. https://operaduo mo.siena.it/la-cattedrale/

Chi Siamo. (n.d.). Santa Maria della Scala. https://www.santa mariadellascala.com/chi-siamo/

Dottor Fabrizio Gabrielli (n.d.). *La psicologia delle contrade del Palio di Siena*. https://www.ilpalio.org/gabrielli_psicologia.htm

Fortezza Medicea di Siena. (n.d.). Visit Tuscany. https://www. visittuscany.com/it/attrazioni/fortezza-medicea-di-siena/

Fortezza Medicea di Siena. (2024c, June 17). Visit Siena Official. https://visitsienaofficial.it/2-fortezza-medicea-di-siena/

Il Duomo di Siena. (n.d.). Visit Tuscany. https://www.visittusc any.com/it/attrazioni/il-duomo-di-siena/

Jack. (n.d.). *la storia – ortodepecci*. La Proposta Cooperative Sociale. http://www.ortodepecci.it/webnew/la-proposta/la-st oria/

La Torre del Mangia. (2024, May 9). Museo Civico Siena. https://museocivico.comune.siena.it/la-torre-del-mangia

La Torre del Mangia. (2024a, February 22). Visit Siena Official. https://visitsienaofficial.it/53-la-torre-del-mangia/

Le mura di Siena. (2023c, September 12). Visit Siena Official. https://visitsienaofficial.it/84-le-mura-di-siena/

L'Orto de' Pecci, il cuore verde di Siena. (n.d.). Visit Tuscany. https://www.visittuscany.com/it/attrazioni/lorto-de-pecci/

Le Porte. (n.d.). *Le Mura di Siena*. Associazione Le Mura di Siena. http://www.lemuradisiena.it/le-mura-di-siena/le-port e/

Origini. (n.d.). Consorzio Tutela Palio di Siena. https://www.c onsorziotutelapaliodisiena.it/index.php/it/le-contrade/origini

Orto botanico. (2024d, September 5). Visit Siena Official. https://visitsienaofficial.it/40-orto-botanico/

PAVIMENTO. (n.d.). Opera Duomo Siena. https://operaduom o.siena.it/pavimento/

Piazza del Campo. (2023d, September 19). Visit Siena Official. https://visitsienaofficial.it/87-piazza-del-campo/

Piazza del Campo. (n.d.). Visit Tuscany. https://www.visittusc any.com/it/attrazioni/piazza-del-campo-siena/

Pinacoteca Nazionale di Siena. (2025, January 3). *Pinacoteca Nazionale - Sito ufficiale della Pinacoteca Nazionale di Siena.* Sito Ufficiale Della Pinacoteca Nazionale Di Siena. https://www.pi nacotecanazionalesiena.it/pinacoteca-nazionale/

PORTA DEL CIELO. (n.d.). Opera Duomo Siena. https://oper aduomo.siena.it/la-porta-del-cielo/

Piazza del Campo. (2024a, January 10). Terre Di Siena. https://www.terredisiena.it/arte-e-cultura/piazza-del-cam po/

Porta giustizia e Orto dei pecci. (2024b, February 27). Visit Siena Official. https://visitsienaofficial.it/91-porta-giustizia-e- orto-dei-pecci/

Torre del Mangia. (2024b, January 10). Terre Di Siena. https://www.terredisiena.it/arte-e-cultura/torre-del-mangia/

Il Duomo di Siena. (2024c, January 11). Terre Di Siena. https://www.terredisiena.it/arte-e-cultura/il-duomo-di-siena /

Musei di Contrada (2023a, July 20). Visit Siena Official. https://visitsienaofficial.it/11-musei-di-contrada/

Veduta dagli Orti de' Tolomei. (2023b, July 24). Visit Siena Official. https://visitsienaofficial.it/72-veduta-dagli-orti-de-t olomei/

VISITA. (n.d.). Opera Duomo Siena. https://operaduomo.siena.it/visita/

Made in the USA
Columbia, SC
06 May 2025